The Tears I Never Cried

Jayne Sevrin-Wright

BookLeaf Publishing

India | USA | UK

Presentation by *BookLeaf Publishing*

Web: www.bookleafpub.com

E-mail: info@bookleafpub.com

ISBN: 9789358319866

First edition 2024

Walking Away

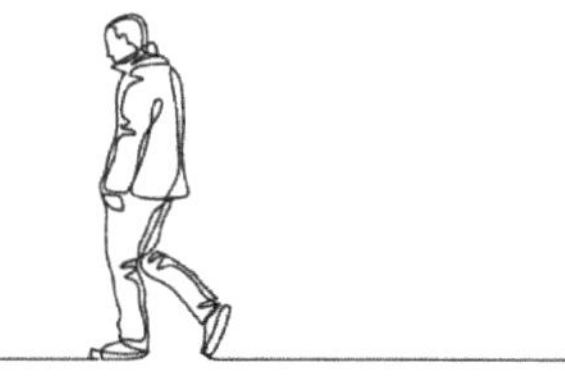

I watched you walk away,
slowly,
becoming a mere fragment
of my used-to-be reality.
Wanting to make you stay
yet knowing
each minute I let you linger,
I'd only die a little more.
Never knew I possessed
the courage
to finally end the madness.
Never knew I'd been
shallow breathing
all this time.
And yet,
For a time and a moment,
I'll still reach out to you,
though you will never see my
outstretched arms.

I'll still call your name,
though you will never hear my voice.
I'll love you still
but you will never,
never know.

Love You With

I love you with my heart,
More with each and every beat
And every breath I take,
I'm more and more complete.

I love you with my dreams,
And with all that they contain.
The wishes and the hopes
Of which you help sustain.

I love you with my soul
Once tired, distressed and torn.
Your love revived its sleeping state,
With your touch, it's reborn.

I love you with my tomorrows,
And a past that brought me here.
I'm intertwined and bound to you.
There's nothing that I fear.

I love you with all that I am.
I have finally been set free.
I will love you till the day I die,
Till I no longer breathe.

Glimpse

A glimpse.
That was all it took,
all that was needed.
Enough to pierce my heart...
short - but long enough for me to
fall again.

2 a.m. letters

2 a.m. love letters,
professing love eternal,
undying affection
and faithful devotion.

2 a.m. hate letters,
questioning fidelity,
suspicious fragility
and damning accusations.

2 a.m. goodbye letters,
expressions of heartache,
feverish reminiscence
and unsure, unwanted farewells.

2 a.m. letters I am tired of writing.

Simple Reminder

Funny how you remember
certain things
because of simple reminders
like the crisp,
cold air
blowing through my window tonight
takes me back
to the
first time
we talked
till 5 a.m.
and I knew
that morning
your voice
would be
a necessity
to my
existence.

Your Voice

In this world of
eternal turmoil,
superficial people
and empty relationships
I have found my solace in your
sweet soothing voice.

Silence

And I loved you in silence
All the while
Knowing
You could never truly be mine
Always hoping
Dreaming
For the day
My day
Under your sun
On the road
To your heart
Wishing each kiss
Each caress
Each waking moment
You shared with her
Was mine.

Knowing realization
Would only be in my dreams
How cruel the fates are
How cold destinys' hand
My love
This love
Only thrives
In silence.

Once More

I know you can hear me
When I cry late at night
When I feel like I'm worn out
And tired of this fight

I know you can see me
And how I live day-to-day
Struggling to survive this
Kneeling to pray

I know you can hear me
When I talk to our son
When I tell him you love him
And how it can't be undone

I know you can see me

Deep down to my core
I would tell you I loved you
If I could see you once more.

Stay

You were never going to stay
I should've realized that
the moment you denied
stealing my heart
and everything else in
my closet of dreams.
Your tempered love danced
upon my hungry heart
with shameful torment.
And I didn't care
The world could fall apart
around me but with you in my life,
I was invincible.
I lived on the edge of danger
forsaking all else
and ignoring all the obvious omens.
You were never going to stay
and then the epiphany after
a long, tumultuous battle
with my conscience...
I finally realized
I was never going to stay either.

Before and After

Before you
I knew there was a sun,
but somehow I never saw it shine.

Before you
I knew a rainbow had different colors
but somehow I only saw gray.

Before you
I knew I could smile
it's just- it ceased to exist on my face.

Before you
I knew I could love
I just never thought I could be loved
like this
by you.

Before you
is a place I never want
to be in ever again.

With you,
Beside you,
Close to you,

This is my...after.

How?

How do you say goodbye?
How do you let go?
How do you forget someone without letting them know?
How do you stop the tears?
How do you move on?
Why does the healing seem so prolonged?
How do you erase memories?
How do you start again?
What will it take for my heart to mend?
How do you end it?
When is the pain enough?
How do you say goodbye to someone you still love?

Far Too Long

How long has it been?
Far too long it seems.
The last time I saw you
Was it only in my dreams?

I remember it all,
The moments we shared,
And I can't help but cry
I can't help but care.

There's a part of me that still needs you
A part of me that yearns
A part that rejects you
A part that has learned.

How I thought love was true,
I thought it had come
But everything's changed
All's said and done.

How long has it been?
Far too long I feel
But now I know what's right
and I finally know what's real.

Soulmates

Between you and I
exists this
love.
One that is
unconditional,
beyond words.
A love
that fills me with
more than anything I can
physically ingest.
A love
that meshes into
and covers
every space,
every crack,
created by

previous loves.

Between you and I
exists a spiritual merge,
an internal weave
of two people
now
called

soulmates.

Unattainable

To live in the haze
of what cannot be
To cry silent tears
of sweet despair
To revel in stolen moments
and uncertainty
To hope in vain
To ache for someone simply
Unattainable.

Left

You left me broken and lost
I live my days in the dark
Sunlight is painful
Smiles are hard

You left me wounded and confused
I spend my nights in solace
Darkness consoles me
Tears are endless

You left me.

HELLO

Here I am standing in the same room with you
    trying to find one witty phrase to utter
Each second that goes by is a missed chance
    I will never get back
Little by little I gather my strength
    and overcome my shyness
Lest I lose this one moment to profess my
    affection for you
One precious moment to tell you:
    I care, I always have...can't you see?

Phone Call

The phone rings
and automatically
without even looking at the screen
I know it's you
I place it on my ear
and your voice confirms it.
You are saddened
by my lack of excitement
and my short answers
confuse you.
You continue anyway,
speaking of the past
as if tears never existed,
as if you were not the one
who walked away.
You speak low
and almost lovingly.

But this time
(guess what?)
I'm no longer listening
My head throbs in pain
My voice filled with rasp.

It's 3 a.m. in the morning
and I don't love you anymore.

Remember

If I am ever in a thought
or memory of yours
I hope that I am remembered
with fondness and even love.
If our lives ever crossed
I hope that I was kind
and loving to you.
If you remember me, I hope you
smile and know how much
you were loved.

After All

Under a sky of starshine
you held me tenderly
and told me that my tears
would no longer fall.

My empty heart became full again
and my chains were broken.
I was mesmerized by your voice
and hypnotized by every word
you wrote to me.

I fantasized, dreamed and then planned
the perfect escape from my mundane life.

I was obsessed and wanted
desperately for you to take me away
But you didn't and couldn't.

You spoke of reality and waking up
and doing what's right
And I hated you.
I turned a deaf ear
and then you were gone.

And it served me right.

After all,

I was already spoken for.

If I Tell You That I Love You

If I tell you that I love you
Would that make you turn away?
Would you hide your face
Avoid my gaze
Be deaf to what I say?

If I tell you that I love you
Would that change the way you smile?
Would you shut me out
And walk away
then say the word goodbye?

If I tell you that I love you
Would that mean our friendship dies?
If that is true,
then I'll be content
to love you with my eyes.

The Guardian in the Sky

"I have to return now."
    he said.
"But I want you to remember
    these words in my stead..."

Smile up at the heavens
Even through the tears.
Love with no abandon
no condition and no fears.

Live every moment
as if it might be the last.
Find happiness in the little things
And let go of the past.

I'll never be too far from you.
I'll watch you from up high.
I will love you beyond forever,
I am your guardian in the sky.

The Search

I searched for your voice
In the vastness of a fading sunset
I looked for your smile
In the face of a thousand moons
I wandered the sands of time
Forever and a day
I looked up to the heavens and prayed
That your memory be burned
And etched into my heart for eternity.

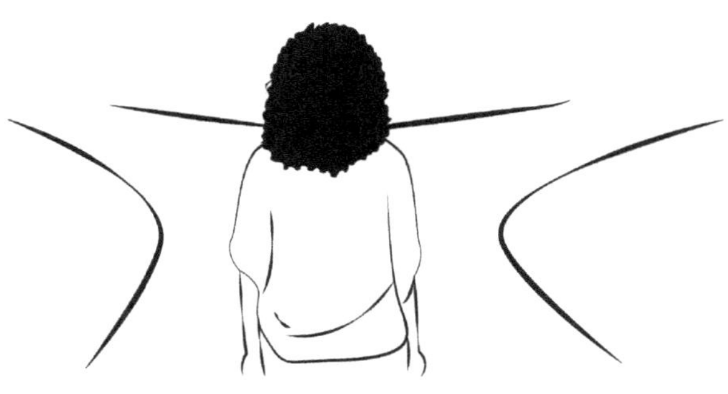

Fade

The warmth in your touch
lessens each day
The light in your eyes
has dimmed
You've become distant
in so many ways
I feel your love slipping
through my fingers
And no matter how much I try
to hold on
To us,
To you
I know I can't for very long
For your silence has weakened me
And my grip.

Eternity

I will meet your memory in the twilight hours
When the world is still asleep

I will steal away into the ether of fallen stars
Where I can quietly mourn our love

I will stand in the whispers of the moonlight
Where my sighs will meet their resting place

In the space between breaths and heartbeats
I will let my tears fall and melt into the air

This love for you is burned into my bones

For eternity.

Suffocate

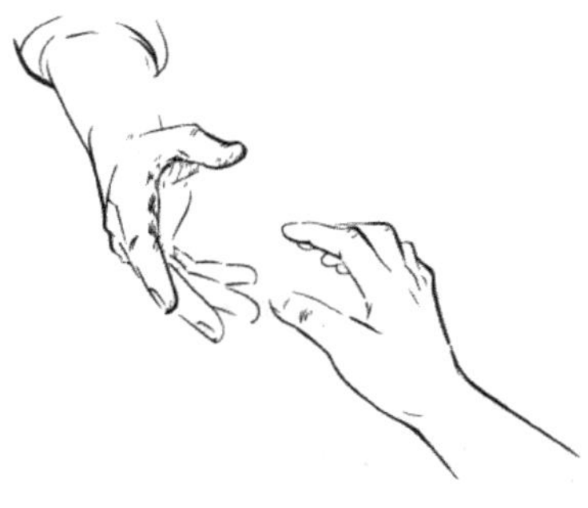

I suffocate in sadness
Inhaling the gray mist
That surrounds me.
I can't taste color.
I can't see what's before me
I can only hear the shallowness
Of my breaths.
My unsettled heart cries
And my will is shattered
And for a moment
Despair has consumed me.
I am bound to this ache
Wanting to be free
And yet I know
If I let go then
I let you go too.

Strong

If you shut your door
I will find the window
If you crawl under a rock
I will overturn boulders
If you hide I will search for you
No matter how deep into the dark you may go
If you turn your back
I will stand in front of you
Again and again
I will hold you closer
Hug you tighter
Love you harder
If only to show you that
I am strong
I can be strong for you
My tears don't mean I've broken down

Or that I've given in
They are merely proof that my love
Is that fierce and unbreakable
I will stand in your black storm
And never let go.

Flatline

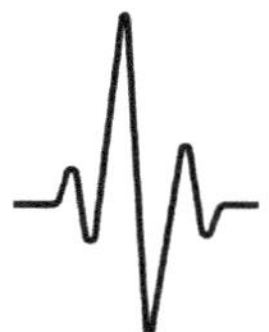

I could close up
Tight.
Impenetrable.
Block you out,
Rid myself
Of this emotion.
Strip completely
Of this pain.
Shut out.
Shut down.
I could throw the key
And destroy the lock.
Let my eyes burn black.
Let my heart flatline.

I'm terrified and sad
That I'm capable
Of such a feat.

Sting

I can still feel the sting of your words
Against my cheek
So many words creating
So much pain
That throbs in my chest
And steals my breath.
But it's the last three
That hurt the most.

I'm sorry.
Goodbye.

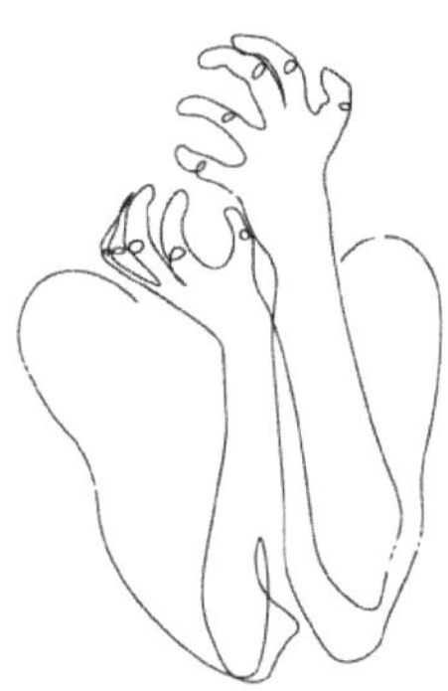

Forbidden

This love I have
I must hold within.
To tell a soul
Is to commit a sin.

NOSTALGIC

N ow and again I return to
O ur once upon a time
S eems like only yesterday when
T ears streamed down my face
A s we walked away from each other
L oneliness has consumed my heart as I
G ather all my strength knowing I have to move
on
I will never stop caring, never stop wondering,
never stop
C herishing your memory.

Where Teardrops Fall

Each time I remember the sadness
It begins to rain inside my soul
My heart collects those streams of hurt
No matter how big or small
And my mind releases the torrent to
This place where teardrops fall.

My Peace

No words need to pass through our lips
We need not exchange phrases nor sentences
Merely a glance,
Simply a look
And your calming presence can lift
The shadows cast on my heart
And for one simple moment
I know peace.

Reunite

And when all is said and done
I will meet you there
In that faraway place
Where pain is no more
And suffering does not exist
Where skies are tranquil
And nature blooms eternal
There, I will meet you
And our souls will reunite in love
Forever.

Something in Your Voice

45

There's something in your voice
That makes me want to tell you
Every little thing,
For no matter what it is,
You will listen and never judge.

There's something in your voice
That calms the turbulence
That sometimes rages within me.

There's something in your voice
That tells me

Your depth is great,
Your heart immense,

And your soul worn…

Just like mine.

I didn't want to hang up.

KISS!

Kiss the sun
Kiss my heart
Kiss the rain
Kiss the dark

Kiss the moon
Kiss the hurt
Kiss the stars
Kiss this thirst

Kiss my soul
Melt the hate
Kiss me, Love
Seal our fate.

The Heart That Saves Me

Your heart never stops saving mine.
Every tear that trickles down my cheeks
Meets its resting place
On your lips,
In your palms.

Your precious ears never tire
Hearing sighs of my past.
Each time I push you away,
You pull me closer,
Hold me tighter
And you blanket me with your strength.

You talk to me

Till the wee hours of the morning,
Just so I am able
To close my eyes and sleep
With some sense of peace.

When I am drowning
In my own breath
Somehow you rescue me
And inflate my soul with your faith.

My oxygen.
My lifejacket.
My rock.

I once existed in gray shadows
Now I bathe in your warm color.

Bittersweet

I stare into your eyes every now and then
Know this: I see forever and I see never.
Bittersweet but sweet nonetheless
Is it me?
Is it you?
Whose heart is beating louder?
At this moment in time,
I think it's mine.
A rush of emotions run through me
Fear, passion, indifference, tenderness.
Sadness and love-
Love?
I don't know how to hold all of this in
It takes my breath away

"Don't let him steal your heart away"

I stare into your eyes every now and then
And I can feel an addiction forming
A hunger
To be touched,
To be held
To be loved by you

I stare into your eyes
Can you see?

Do you know?

"Don't let him steal your heart away"

My palm holds an imprint of your sweet kiss.
I close my hand and pray
That it doesn't fade too soon.

The Lesson I Will Never Learn

You're the ache that never ends
And the pain that radiates throughout my days
You're the shallow breaths I try to take
And the exhales heavy with sorrow.

You're the sadness so transparent in my eyes
And the emptiness that lives in my heart
You're the love I keep taking back
Knowing it will only hurt me again.

You're the lesson I will never learn.